# Helicopters

## Emily Bone

Designed by Zoe Wray
and Steve Wood

Illustrated by Staz Johnson, Giovanni Paulli
and Adrian Roots

Edited by Alex Frith
Helicopter expert: Mac Macarthy

# Contents

This is an MD 500 helicopter, which is carrying a film crew filming a surfer in Hawaii, USA.

Helicopters are uniquely suited to this kind of work, as they can fly very close to the waves and follow the surfer's moves.

# Amazing flying machines

Unlike most planes, helicopters can take off vertically, without a runway, and fly and land almost anywhere. They can rush to emergencies, whisk soldiers off the battlefield, and even attack enemy targets.

### Basic parts of a helicopter

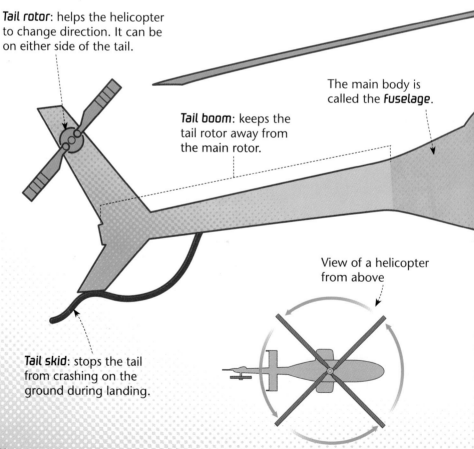

**Tail rotor**: helps the helicopter to change direction. It can be on either side of the tail.

**Tail boom**: keeps the tail rotor away from the main rotor.

The main body is called the **fuselage**.

View of a helicopter from above

**Tail skid**: stops the tail from crashing on the ground during landing.

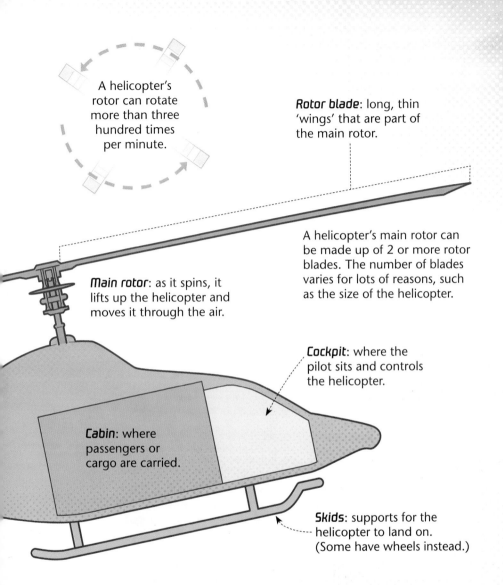

A helicopter's rotor can rotate more than three hundred times per minute.

**Rotor blade**: long, thin 'wings' that are part of the main rotor.

A helicopter's main rotor can be made up of 2 or more rotor blades. The number of blades varies for lots of reasons, such as the size of the helicopter.

**Main rotor**: as it spins, it lifts up the helicopter and moves it through the air.

**Cockpit**: where the pilot sits and controls the helicopter.

**Cabin**: where passengers or cargo are carried.

**Skids**: supports for the helicopter to land on. (Some have wheels instead.)

## Helicopter crew

- **Pilot**: flies the helicopter.
- **Co-pilot**: sits next to the pilot. Has controls to take over from the pilot if necessary.

In some helicopters:
- **Observer**: acts as a look-out and guides the pilot, especially in bad weather.

# Different designs

From small pilot-training helicopters, to huge army transporters, helicopters are specially designed for different jobs.

### Transport and emergency helicopters

Length of fuselage from nose to tail ----

Distance that the helicopter can fly without taking in more fuel ----

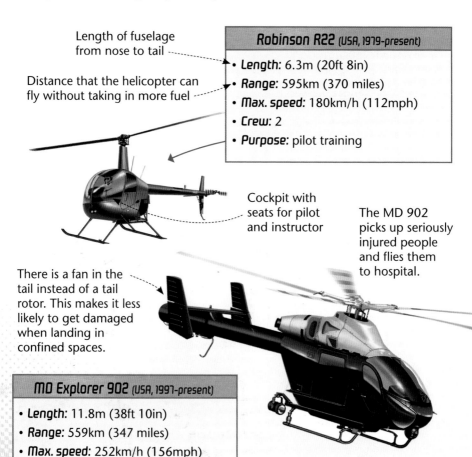

**Robinson R22** (USA, 1979-present)

- **Length:** 6.3m (20ft 8in)
- **Range:** 595km (370 miles)
- **Max. speed:** 180km/h (112mph)
- **Crew:** 2
- **Purpose:** pilot training

Cockpit with seats for pilot and instructor

The MD 902 picks up seriously injured people and flies them to hospital.

There is a fan in the tail instead of a tail rotor. This makes it less likely to get damaged when landing in confined spaces.

**MD Explorer 902** (USA, 1997-present)

- **Length:** 11.8m (38ft 10in)
- **Range:** 559km (347 miles)
- **Max. speed:** 252km/h (156mph)
- **Crew:** 2
- **Purpose:** air ambulance, police patrol

News reporters broadcast live reports from the helicopter.

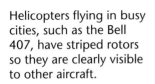

Helicopters flying in busy cities, such as the Bell 407, have striped rotors so they are clearly visible to other aircraft.

### Bell 407 *(USA, 1996–present)*

- **Length:** 12.7m (41ft 8in)
- **Range:** 598km (372 miles)
- **Max. speed:** 260km/h (161mph)
- **Capacity:** 1 crew and 5 passengers
- **Purpose:** passenger transport

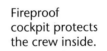

Fireproof cockpit protects the crew inside.

Water-filled tank is emptied on the fire.

### S-70 Firehawk *(USA, 1979–present)*

- **Length:** 16.7m (54ft 9in)
- **Range:** 361km (224 miles)
- **Max. speed:** 276km/h (171mph)
- **Crew:** 2
- **Purpose:** firefighting

## SH-3 Sea King (USA, 1961-present)

- **Length:** 19.76m (64ft 10in)
- **Range:** 1,000km (621 miles)
- **Max. speed:** 267km/h (166mph)
- **Capacity:** 4 crew and 3 passengers
- **Purpose:** naval search and rescue, anti-submarine warfare

The Sea King carries equipment for detecting and locating enemy submarines.

The tail rotor is enclosed in the tail. This is called a fenestron. It protects the rotor from damage by weapons.

OH-1 Kawasaki helicopters fly into enemy territory and bring back information.

## OH-1 Kawasaki (Japan, 2000-present)

- **Length:** 12m (39ft 4in)
- **Range:** 540km (336 miles)
- **Max. speed:** 278km/h (173mph)
- **Crew:** 2
- **Purpose:** army scout helicopter

### Denel AH2 Rooivalk (South Africa, 1999-present)

- **Length:** 18.73m (61ft 5in)
- **Range:** 1,130km (700 miles)
- **Max. speed:** 309km/h (193mph)
- **Crew:** 2
- **Purpose:** army attack helicopter

Two cockpits: one for the pilot and one for the co-pilot

Cannon

Rockets and missiles are mounted on the sides of the helicopter. Find out more on pages 24-27.

# Cargo and heavy lift helicopters

Two main rotors positioned side by side make this helicopter very powerful.

The K-1200 lifts tree trunks from where they have been cut down. The trunks are carried in a sling underneath the helicopter.

## Kaman K-1200 (USA, 1999-present)

- **Length:** 15.8m (51ft 10in)
- **Range:** 494.5km (307 miles)
- **Max. speed:** 185.2km/h (115mph)
- **Crew:** 1
- **Max. cargo weight:** 2,722kg (6,000lbs)
- **Purpose:** lifting heavy loads

### Boeing Vertol CH-113 (USA, 1964-2004)

- **Length:** 25.7m (84ft 4in)
- **Range:** 1,100km (690 miles)
- **Max. speed:** 274km/h (170mph)
- **Capacity:** 5 crew and 26 passengers
- **Purpose:** cargo transport and sea search and rescue

Rotors positioned at either end of fuselage, known as tandem rotors.

Boat-shaped, waterproof fuselage so the helicopter can land on water.

### Kamov KA-32 (Russia, 1964-present)

- **Length:** 11.3m (37ft)
- **Range:** 676km (420 miles)
- **Max. speed:** 265km/h (165mph)
- **Crew:** 5
- **Purpose:** cargo transport

Two main rotors are placed on top of each other.

# In the cockpit

A helicopter can turn instantly to fly in any direction. The pilot controls it using both hands and both feet at once to move levers and pedals in the cockpit.

This is the cockpit of an AW109 Power helicopter.

# The Apache

The AH-64D Apache Longbow is one of the latest, state-of-the-art army attack helicopters. It can destroy enemy tanks, engage in air-to-air battles, and provide back-up for troops on the ground.

Here, Apache Longbows are being built in a manufacturing plant in Arizona, USA. The US army has more than 800 Apaches currently in service. They are also sold to armed forces around the world.

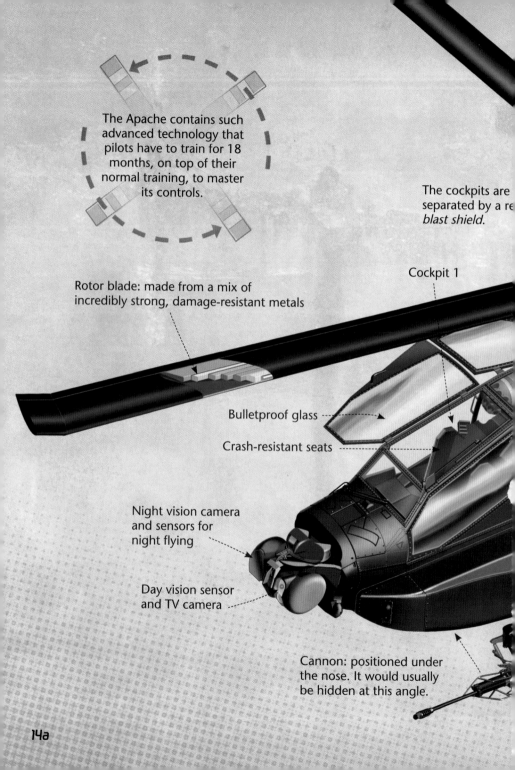

The Apache contains such advanced technology that pilots have to train for 18 months, on top of their normal training, to master its controls.

The cockpits are separated by a re *blast shield*.

Cockpit 1

Rotor blade: made from a mix of incredibly strong, damage-resistant metals

Bulletproof glass

Crash-resistant seats

Night vision camera and sensors for night flying

Day vision sensor and TV camera

Cannon: positioned under the nose. It would usually be hidden at this angle.

Dome containing radar system – for detecting and identifying enemy targets

Engine

nforced

Cockpit 2

Cutaway to show engine

The Apache has an engine on each side so that the helicopter can fly if one engine fails.

Stub wings carry weapons and missiles. They also store extra fuel.

U.S. ARMY

ARMY

Missiles

Rocket launcher

Landing wheels

Cockpit

There are seats in the cockpit for the pilot and co-pilot. Some controls are duplicated so that the co-pilot can take over flying the helicopter without switching sides.

## Cockpit controls

Here's what the different controls do:

❶ Collective stick: makes the helicopter move up and down.

❷ Cyclic stick: tilts the main rotor, making the helicopter fly forward, back, or to the side.

❸ Yaw foot pedals: control the tail rotor to rotate the helicopter to the left or right.

❹ Moving map display: shows where the helicopter is on an electronic map.

❺ Airspeed indicator: tells the pilot how fast the helicopter is flying.

❻ Artificial horizon: shows if the helicopter's nose is dipping down to the horizon or pointing up, helping the pilot to fly straight.

The co-pilot has a collective stick of his own, but it is out of the picture, here.

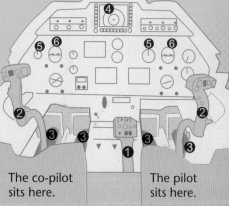

The co-pilot sits here.

The pilot sits here.

h

ings keep the tail
during flight.

The main
rotor has four
blades.

Length of
helicopter
(from nose to
tail): 17.73m
(58.2ft)

## Inside the cockpits

### Cockpit 1
This is where the gunner sits. He detects
and fires at enemy targets. Video screens
show footage from cameras and sensors on
the Apache's nose.

Screen for enemy
target detection
and tracking

Hand grips for
selecting and
firing weapons

Radar and
navigation
data

### Cockpit 2
The pilot sits here, behind cockpit 1. This
cockpit is raised up so the pilot can see clearly
out of the front of the helicopter.

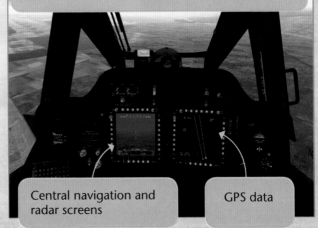

Central navigation and
radar screens

GPS data

Global Positioning System (GPS) antenna: a system for navigation using satellites and computers

LJ211

Tail rotor w
four blades

Tail \
stab

The tail wheel stops the tail from being damaged in landing.

DANGER

Strong metal shaft for turning the powerful tail rotor

This symbol means that the helicopter is flown by Britain's Royal Air Force.

Main rotor

Each blade is 7.3m (24ft) long.

## AH-64D Apache Longbow
### (USA, 1997-present)

- **Range:** 482km (300 miles)
- **Max. speed:** 284km/h (176mph)
- **Weight:** 5,352kg (11,800lb)
- **Crew:** 2: pilot and gunner
- **Weapons:** missiles, rockets and shells

# Attack helicopters

Here are some more modern attack helicopters. In each one, the pilot is accompanied by a gunner.

## Mi-24 Hind (Russia, 1976-present)

- **Length:** 20m (65ft)
- **Range:** 750km (465 miles)
- **Max. speed:** 310km/h (192mph)
- **Weapons:** rockets, missiles, bullets and bombs

Bulletproof fuselage and cockpit glass

Large cabin to transport up to 8 soldiers

Machine gun

Rocket launcher

Anti-tank missiles

## KA-50 Black Shark (Russia, 1995-present)

- **Length:** 13.5m (44ft)
- **Range:** 1160km (720 miles)
- **Max. speed:** 390km/h (242mph)
- **Weapons:** missiles, rockets, shells and bombs

Attack helicopters always have a crew of two, sitting in *tandem cockpits* (one in front of the other).

No tail rotor

Two main rotors make the helicopter faster.

Missiles

Cannon

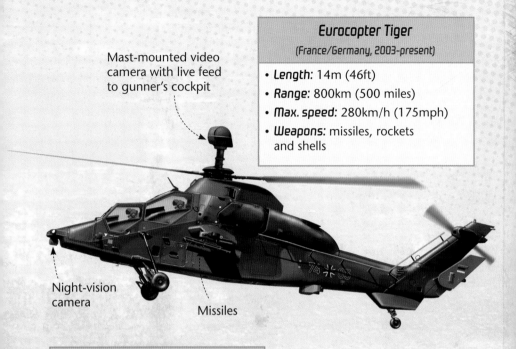

Mast-mounted video camera with live feed to gunner's cockpit

## Eurocopter Tiger
### (France/Germany, 2003-present)

- **Length:** 14m (46ft)
- **Range:** 800km (500 miles)
- **Max. speed:** 280km/h (175mph)
- **Weapons:** missiles, rockets and shells

Night-vision camera

Missiles

## W2-10 (China, 2003-present)

- **Length:** 14m (46ft)
- **Range:** 800km (500 miles)
- **Max. speed:** 270km/h (168mph)
- **Weapons:** missiles, rockets, bullets and grenades

Rocket launcher and missiles

Machine gun

# Scouting missions

Before an attack helicopter enters enemy territory, small, fast helicopters fly in first. Known as scout helicopters, they gather important information, such as the position and firepower of enemy troops.

Scouts fly in pairs – if one is shot down, the other can continue the mission.

Mast-mounted sight

### Bell OH-58D Kiowa (USA, 1962-present)

- **Length:** 10m (33ft)
- **Range:** 556km (345 miles)
- **Max. speed:** 222km/h (138mph)
- **Crew:** 2
- **Weapons:** missiles, rockets and bullets

Behind enemy lines...

...the helicopters fly very low to the ground, making it difficult for radar to detect them.

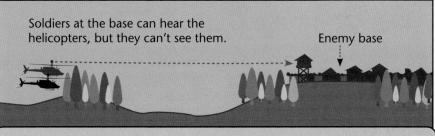

Soldiers at the base can hear the helicopters, but they can't see them.

Enemy base

About 8km (5 miles) from an enemy base, the helicopters hover behind trees. Their cameras stick up above the tree tops and zoom in on the base.

A screen in the cockpit shows a close-up view of the base. The co-pilot records enemy troop numbers and weapons.

6 armed enemy personnel; 2 tanks; buildings occupied...

# Military transporters

Fast, powerful and with a large cabin space, army transport helicopters fly military personnel and supplies straight to the battlefield.

## Chinook

Chinooks are commonly used for military transport. Up to 55 soldiers can be carried inside a Chinook's cabin.

They also pick up wounded soldiers and fly them to a hospital.

Troops enter and exit the helicopter through a rear cabin door.

If an aircraft crashes in a remote or dangerous area, Chinooks can quickly pick up crew members and even collect the wreckage.

Two tandem main rotors and no tail create a long, wide cabin area for transporting soldiers and cargo.

Machine guns mounted on either side can be used if landing in enemy territory.

Loads can also be carried, or 'slung', from long cables underneath the Chinook.

This helicopter is moving a military truck.

## CH-47 Chinook (USA 1962-present)

- **Length:** 15.54m (51ft)
- **Range:** 741km (450 miles)
- **Max. speed:** 298km/h (185mph)
- **Crew:** 4
- **Weapons:** bullets

## How much can it carry?

- **Inside the cabin:** 55 soldiers (or 33 soldiers plus equipment), 24 stretchers, 2 military trucks
- **Hanging cargo:** 4,536kg (10,000lbs)

# Army giants

The CH-53 Super Stallion and the Mil Mi-26 Halo
are two of the biggest helicopters around today.
Like the Chinook, they are used for army transport.

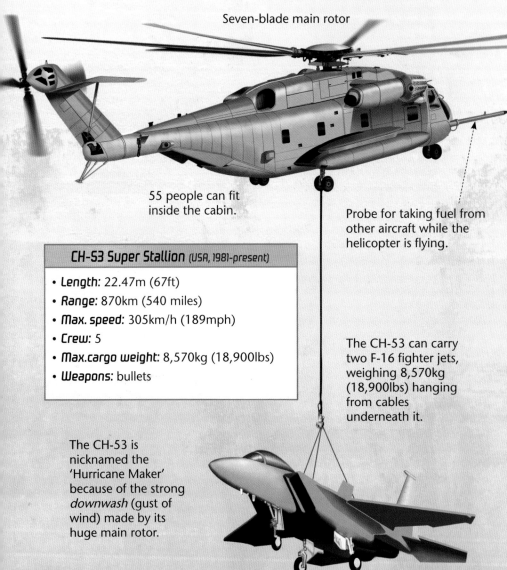

Seven-blade main rotor

55 people can fit
inside the cabin.

Probe for taking fuel from
other aircraft while the
helicopter is flying.

## CH-53 Super Stallion (USA, 1981-present)

- **Length:** 22.47m (67ft)
- **Range:** 870km (540 miles)
- **Max. speed:** 305km/h (189mph)
- **Crew:** 5
- **Max.cargo weight:** 8,570kg (18,900lbs)
- **Weapons:** bullets

The CH-53 can carry
two F-16 fighter jets,
weighing 8,570kg
(18,900lbs) hanging
from cables
underneath it.

The CH-53 is
nicknamed the
'Hurricane Maker'
because of the strong
*downwash* (gust of
wind) made by its
huge main rotor.

## Mil Mi-26 Halo *(Russia, 1983-present)*

- **Length:** 33.73m (110ft 7in)
- **Range:** 800km (497 miles)
- **Max. speed:** 295km/h (183mph)
- **Crew:** 6
- **Max. cargo weight:** 24,000kg (53,000lbs)
- **Weapons:** none

Main rotor has eight blades.

The huge cabin is big enough to transport up to 90 people.

## Length comparison

Mil Mi-26 Halo
33.72m (110ft 7in)

Apache AH-64D
17.73m (58.2ft)

CH-53 Super Stallion
22.47m (67ft)

CH-47 Chinook
15.54m (51ft)

23

# Firepower

Most attack helicopters are armed with rockets, shells and missiles. These all explode on impact, seriously damaging enemy targets.

## Rockets

Rockets are aimed by the gunner, then fired out of a rocket launcher at targets on the ground. Here's how they work:

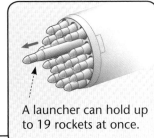

A launcher can hold up to 19 rockets at once.

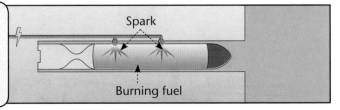

1. The gunner presses a switch to connect with one rocket in the rocket launcher.

An electrical charge is sent through the rocket launcher, into the rocket.

Electrical charge

Rocket launcher

Rocket

Explosive tip

Chamber of rocket filled with fuel

2. This creates a spark that lights the fuel chamber in the rocket.

Spark

Burning fuel

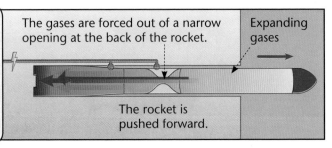

3. Burning fuel creates expanding gases that are pushed out of the back of the rocket. This propels the rocket forward.

The gases are forced out of a narrow opening at the back of the rocket.

Expanding gases

The rocket is pushed forward.

**Gunner**
Aims and fires the weapons.

**Rocket launcher**
Holds rockets in tubes until they are fired.

**Missiles**
See pages 26-27.

**Cannon**
A gun that fires shells when close to target.

# Cannons

A cannon fires small explosives, called shells, at targets on the ground. The shells are fed into the barrel from a chain, and shot out at a rate of 12 per second.

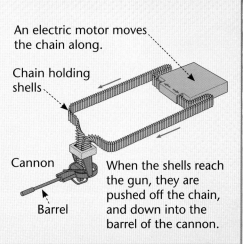

An electric motor moves the chain along.

Chain holding shells

Cannon

Barrel

When the shells reach the gun, they are pushed off the chain, and down into the barrel of the cannon.

# Guided missiles

Helicopter Fire and Forget, or Hellfire, missiles have a built-in radar seeker to locate targets. They can destroy large objects on the ground, such as tanks and buildings.

## How Hellfire missiles work

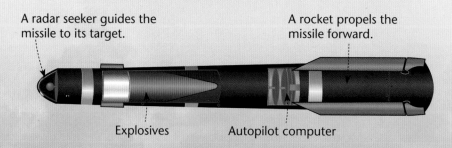

A radar seeker guides the missile to its target.

A rocket propels the missile forward.

Explosives

Autopilot computer

This SH-60F Sea Hawk helicopter has just launched a Hellfire missile. It takes a maximum of 19.2 seconds to reach a target 8km (5 miles) away.

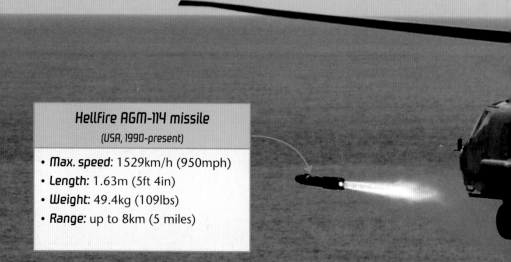

### Hellfire AGM-114 missile
(USA, 1990-present)

- **Max. speed:** 1529km/h (950mph)
- **Length:** 1.63m (5ft 4in)
- **Weight:** 49.4kg (109lbs)
- **Range:** up to 8km (5 miles)

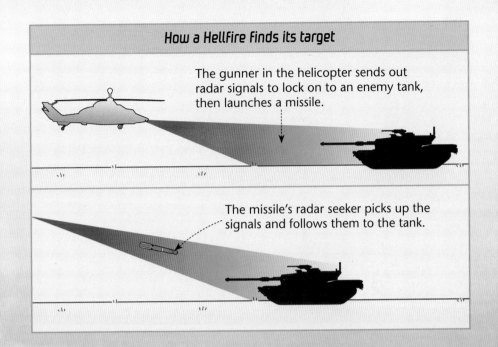

## How a Hellfire finds its target

The gunner in the helicopter sends out radar signals to lock on to an enemy tank, then launches a missile.

The missile's radar seeker picks up the signals and follows them to the tank.

# Ready, aim, fire

An Apache gunner is looking for a store of enemy weapons he has been ordered to destroy. He uses radar to search for targets up to 8km (5 miles) away. Radar systems send out signals to find far-away objects.

Radar

Pilot

Gunner

The gunner will attack the target with shells.

The radar detects what different objects are. This information is then sent to a radar screen in the gunner's cockpit.

Buildings

Missile launchers

Vehicles

When the helicopter is close to the target, the gunner slides a computer screen in front of his eye. This gives him a more direct, realistic view.

Enemy missile launcher

A camera on the front of the helicopter zooms in on the target. The images are sent to the gunner's computer screen.

A cross on the screen shows where the cannon is pointing.

The gunner activates the cannon. It is linked to the movement of his helmet, so when he turns his head the cannon moves, too.

BOOM!!

The gunner looks in the direction he wants to fire the cannon.

When he has aimed the cannon, the gunner pushes a button to fire it.

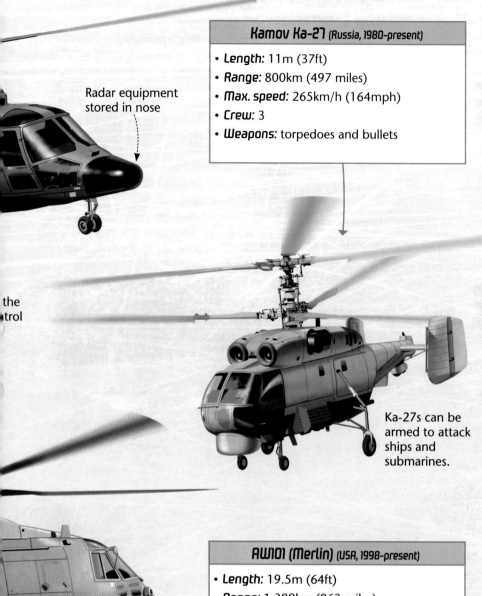

Radar equipment
stored in nose

## Kamov Ka-27 *(Russia, 1980-present)*

- **Length:** 11m (37ft)
- **Range:** 800km (497 miles)
- **Max. speed:** 265km/h (164mph)
- **Crew:** 3
- **Weapons:** torpedoes and bullets

the
trol

Ka-27s can be
armed to attack
ships and
submarines.

## AW101 (Merlin) *(USA, 1998-present)*

- **Length:** 19.5m (64ft)
- **Range:** 1,389km (863 miles)
- **Max. speed:** 309km/h (192mph)
- **Crew:** 3-4
- **Weapons:** missiles, torpedoes, depth
  charges and bullets

Radar scanner

A version of the AS 565, called the Z-9, is made for Chinese military forces.

## Eurocopter AS565 Panther (France, 1972-present)

- **Length:** 12m (39ft)
- **Range:** 880km (547 miles)
- **Max. speed:** 296km/h (184mph)
- **Crew:** 2
- **Weapons:** missiles, torpedoes and bullets

Two main rotors make helicopter easier to co in strong sea winds.

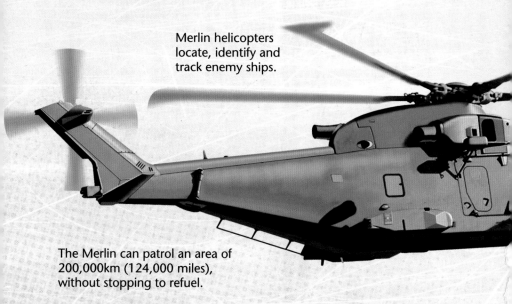

Merlin helicopters locate, identify and track enemy ships.

The Merlin can patrol an area of 200,000km (124,000 miles), without stopping to refuel.

# All at sea

Naval helicopters drop off supplies, transport people safely from ship to ship, and patrol the sea, looking out for enemy vessels.

The blades of the main rotor on this helicopter have been folded back so that it can be stowed away on the ship.

**Westland Sea King HAS 6** (USA, 1994-present)

- **Length:** 17.3m (57ft)
- **Range:** 1230km (764 miles)
- **Max. speed:** 230km/h (143mph)
- **Crew:** 3
- **Weapons:** torpedoes, depth charges (see pages 32-35 to find out more)

This Sea King HAS 6 helicopter is landing on the deck of an assault ship – a base for naval troops at sea.

'Balloons' under the stub wings inflate so the helicopter floats if it lands on water.

Wide, double-door on cabin allows troops to climb out quickly.

Cargo is winched down to ship's deck.

## CH-46 Sea Knight (USA, 1964-present)

- **Length:** 13.92m (46ft)
- **Range:** 676km (420 miles)
- **Max. speed:** 265km/h (165mph)
- **Crew:** 5 (including observer and gunner)
- **Weapons:** bullets

## MH-60S Knight Hawk (USA, 2000-present)

- **Length:** 19.8m (65ft)
- **Range:** 447km (278 miles)
- **Max. speed:** 268km/h (167mph)
- **Crew:** 4
- **Weapons:** missiles, torpedoes, bullets

Cabin space for 25
fully-equipped soldiers

# Sub hunters

Some naval helicopters are equipped to hunt out and attack submarines. They are known as anti-submarine warfare (ASW) helicopters.

This Super Lynx helicopter is dropping a weapon called a depth charge into the water. When it sinks and reaches a certain depth, it will explode.

Depth charge

### Super Lynx (USA, 1994-present)

- **Length:** 13.33m (44ft)
- **Range:** 590km (365 miles)
- **Max. speed:** 322km/h (200mph)
- **Crew:** 2 plus up to 7 flight engineers
- **Weapons:** missiles, torpedoes and depth charges

ASW helicopters use dipping sonar to detect subs by listening out for them. See pages 34-35 to find out how this works.

ASW helicopters are teamed with a naval ship. As well as hunting subs, they transport troops and supplies, and undertake search and rescue missions.

The Lynx spends a long time flying out at sea without anywhere to land. There is a team of flight engineers on every flight to fix any problems in the air.

## ASW helicopter weapons

### Sea Skua missile

Contains a radar seeker which locates and locks onto large ships. Explodes on impact.

### Stingray torpedo

Missile that is dropped into the water to destroy subs. An on-board computer locates and directs the torpedo to its target.

# How dipping sonar works

Dipping sonar is lowered by ASW helicopters into the sea. It contains an underwater microphone, or hydrophone, that picks up sounds underwater.

Hydrophones are so sensitive they can hear a hammer being dropped inside a submarine deep underwater.

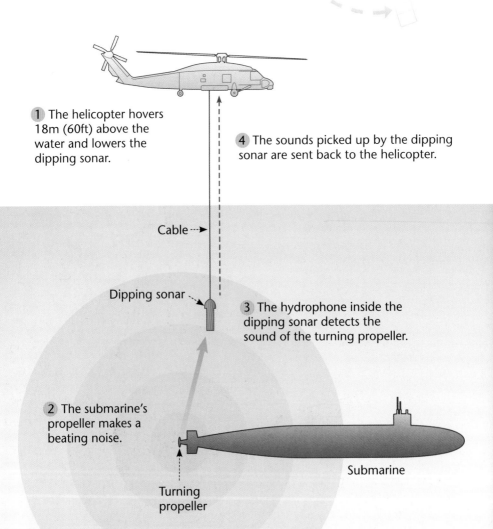

1 The helicopter hovers 18m (60ft) above the water and lowers the dipping sonar.

4 The sounds picked up by the dipping sonar are sent back to the helicopter.

Cable ---▶

Dipping sonar ---

3 The hydrophone inside the dipping sonar detects the sound of the turning propeller.

2 The submarine's propeller makes a beating noise.

Submarine

Turning propeller

## The sonar operator

- The sounds from the sonar are converted into lines on a computer screen.

- A sonar operator studies the lines, which tell him where the submarine is.

Sonar operator

The operator can also hear the sounds through headphones.

# Dropping a depth charge

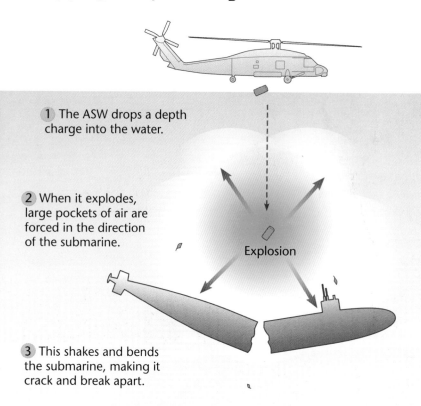

1 The ASW drops a depth charge into the water.

2 When it explodes, large pockets of air are forced in the direction of the submarine.

Explosion

3 This shakes and bends the submarine, making it crack and break apart.

# Staying safe

Helicopters flying in combat zones are always at risk of being attacked. But they have various types of equipment to stop missiles from finding them.

The helicopter is firing out flares, which confuse heat-seeking missiles, missiles that find a target by detecting its heat.

This HH-60H Sea Hawk helicopter is used to rescue soldiers who have had an accident at sea, often within enemy territory.

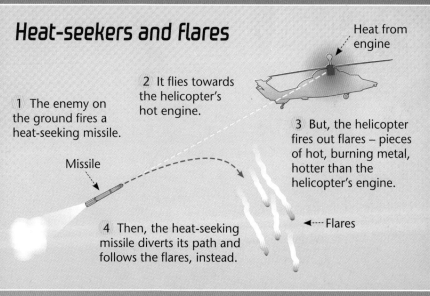

## Heat-seekers and flares

Heat from engine

1 The enemy on the ground fires a heat-seeking missile.

2 It flies towards the helicopter's hot engine.

3 But, the helicopter fires out flares – pieces of hot, burning metal, hotter than the helicopter's engine.

Missile

4 Then, the heat-seeking missile diverts its path and follows the flares, instead.

Flares

# Chaff

Some helicopters fire out chaff – a cloud of tiny metal or glass fragments that interferes with enemy radar systems.

Chaff spreads out around the helicopter after it's fired out.

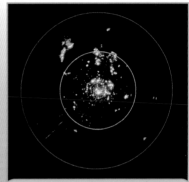

The chaff shows up as dots and blotches on a radar screen. A helicopter inside the area can't be identified.

## Nap of the Earth flight

Another way to avoid detection by enemy radar is to fly through valleys or behind trees.

Enemy radar

The enemy's radar signal is blocked by the sides of the valley.

This technique is called Nap of the Earth as it comes from the French word *nappe* which means covering.

Area out of radar's range

# Exhaust cooling

Cooling systems are designed to cover up the trail of hot gases left behind by a helicopter's engine.

This helicopter's exhaust – the hot gas pumped out by its engine – can be detected by heat-seeking missiles.

This helicopter has a cooling system, which mixes cold air with the hot exhaust. This makes the exhaust harder to detect.

# Radar jamming

Jammers make it difficult for radar-guided missiles to detect a helicopter's position.

1. A radar jamming device on the helicopter sends out strong, decoy radar signals.

Decoy radar signal

2. Missile is launched and starts to fly towards the helicopter.

3. But then a radar scanner on the missile detects the decoy signals.

4. The missile is thrown off course, away from the helicopter.

# Behind enemy lines

Sometimes, MH-60G Pave Hawk helicopters fly troops on missions in enemy territory. They can drop off soldiers quickly and safely, without being attacked by the enemy.

Strong rotor blades can withstand hits by shells and bullets.

Window-mounted guns

## MH-60G Pave Hawk (USA, 1991-present)

- **Length:** 17.38m (57ft)
- **Range:** 964km (600 miles)
- **Max. speed:** 296km/h (183mph)
- **Crew:** 5
- **Weapons:** bullets

This probe allows the helicopter to take fuel from another aircraft while flying.

A terrain-following radar system allows the Pave Hawk to fly safely, very low to the ground. This avoids detection by enemy radar.

An on-board computer automatically adjusts the helicopter's height so it flies over obstacles.

The helicopter hovers close to the ground. Rope ladders are dropped down from cabin doors and the soldiers quickly climb down them.

Gunners fire bullets to keep enemy forces away from the soldiers.

As the helicopter flies away, it fires out flares and chaff so missiles can't track it down.

# The Second World War

Helicopters were used on the battlefield for the first time during the Second World War – for observation and evacuation of injured soldiers.

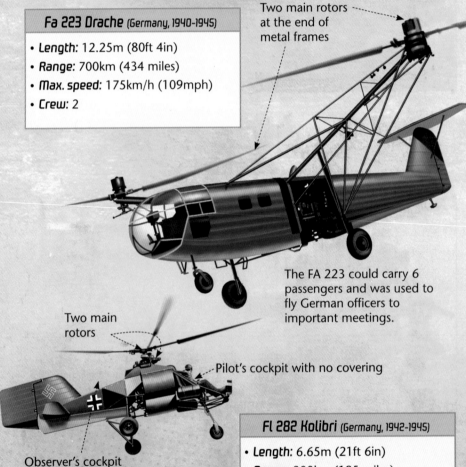

### Fa 223 Drache (Germany, 1940-1945)

- **Length:** 12.25m (80ft 4in)
- **Range:** 700km (434 miles)
- **Max. speed:** 175km/h (109mph)
- **Crew:** 2

Two main rotors at the end of metal frames

The FA 223 could carry 6 passengers and was used to fly German officers to important meetings.

Two main rotors

Pilot's cockpit with no covering

Observer's cockpit

### Fl 282 Kolibri (Germany, 1942-1945)

- **Length:** 6.65m (21ft 6in)
- **Range:** 300km (185 miles)
- **Max. speed:** 150km/h (93mph)
- **Crew:** 1

Working closely with the German Navy, FL 282s carried equipment between ships.

The wide cockpit could seat the pilot and an observer.

The R-4 was the first helicopter to be made on a factory production line. Over 130 were built.

A later model, the R-5, had a more powerful engine than the R-4, which gave it a longer range. It was used after the war for mail transport across the USA.

## Sikorsky R-4 (USA, 1939-1944)

- **Length:** 10.2m (33ft 8in)
- **Range:** 209km (130 miles)
- **Max. speed:** 120km/h (74mph)
- **Crew:** 1

## Sikorsky S-51 (USA, 1944-1951)

- **Length:** 12.5m (41ft 2in)
- **Range:** 450km (280 miles)
- **Max. speed:** 145km/h (90mph)
- **Crew:** 1

Two cases for holding stretchers could be fitted on either side of the fuselage.

This Bell H-13 helicopter has rescued an injured soldier at sea, and is taking him to an army hospital on a ship.

Two fixed 'wings' under the main rotor give the helicopter extra lift.

The H-13 had no cabin, so injured people were loaded onto stretcher cases outside the helicopter.

Helicopters used in the Korean War were nicknamed 'choppers' because their two-blade rotors made a 'chop chop' sound.

NAVY
128915

# The Korean War

During the Korean War (1950-1953), helicopters flew seriously injured soldiers to army hospitals so they could be given emergency treatment.

Bubble cockpit gave pilot clear, all-round view while flying.

Everyone around the helicopter is bending down to avoid the spinning rotor blades.

A doctor always flew with the pilot, so he could give first aid at the scene.

## Bell H-13 (USA, 1945-1960)

- **Length:** 9.63m (31ft)
- **Range:** 383km (240 miles)
- **Max. speed:** 161km/h (100mph)
- **Crew:** 2

# The Vietnam War

Helicopters played a major role in the Vietnam War (1955-1975), moving troops and supplies rapidly across areas covered in thick jungle.

## First helicopter weapons

The Bell UH-1 helicopter (nicknamed 'Huey') was the first helicopter to use guns to attack targets on the ground.

Large cabin could carry up to 10 soldiers or six stretchers.

A gunner fired shells from a machine gun strapped to the helicopter.

### Bell UH-1 Iroquois Huey (USA, 1959-present)

- **Length:** 12.31m (40ft 5in)
- **Range:** 383km (237 miles)
- **Speed:** 204km/h (126mph)
- **Crew:** 3
- **Weapons:** bullets

Here, a gunner in a UH-1 watches an HH-53C helicopter fly past. HH-53Cs rescued injured soldiers, and transported troops and supplies.

## HH-53C *(USA, 1966-present)*

- **Length:** 20.47m (67ft)
- **Range:** 868km (540 miles)
- **Max. speed:** 315km/h (196mph)
- **Crew:** 6, including 2 flight engineers
- **Weapons:** bullets

# Jungle attack

From the 1960s, attack helicopters, such as the AH-1G Cobra, had built-in machine guns and rocket launchers. They always flew with an OH-6A Cayuse, a smaller, faster observation helicopter.

## AH-1G Cobra (USA, 1967-present)

- **Length:** 16.26m (53ft 4in)
- **Range:** 574km (357 miles)
- **Max. speed:** 277km/h (172mph)
- **Crew:** 2
- **Weapons:** rockets, grenades and bullets

AH-1G Cobras were armed with rockets and grenades to destroy enemy targets.

A gunner fired weapons using controls in the cockpit.

The Cayuse was known as the 'flying egg' because of its oval fuselage.

## OH-6A Cayuse (USA, 1963-present)

- **Length:** 9.4m (30ft 10in)
- **Range:** 430km (267 miles)
- **Max. speed:** 282km/h (175mph)
- **Crew:** 2
- **Weapons:** bullets

The Cayuse flew very low to the ground, so an observer inside could look out for enemy camps.

When the observer in the Cayuse spotted an enemy camp, he fired a smoke grenade.

The smoke showed the Cobra's crew the position of the camp.

The Cayuse quickly hid by flying down behind trees.

Then, the gunner in the Cobra fired a rocket in the direction of the smoke. As the rockets exploded, the Cobra turned around and flew to safety.

# The Gulf War

During the Gulf War (1990-1991), Black Hawk helicopters carried troops quickly across the deserts and mountains of Iraq.

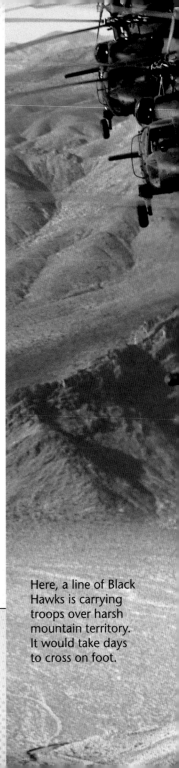

---

### UH-60A Black Hawk (USA, 1979-present)

- **Length:** 19.76m (65ft)
- **Range:** 600km (370 miles)
- **Max. speed:** 296km/h (184mph)
- **Capacity:** 4 crew and up to 11 soldiers
- **Weapons:** missiles, rockets and bullets

---

Black Hawks were much faster than earlier helicopters. This made them less exposed to enemy attack.

Here, a line of Black Hawks is carrying troops over harsh mountain territory. It would take days to cross on foot.

As the helicopter hovered just above the ground, fully armed soldiers jumped out through wide cabin doors, ready for action.

# Emergency helicopters

Helicopters are incredibly flexible about where they can fly and land, making them vital for emergency services.

## Firefighting

Firefighting helicopters carry tanks or buckets filled with water, chemicals or foam.

### Putting out the fire

1. Hovering over a lake, the pilot of this Firehawk S-70 helicopter lowers a snorkel into the water.

2. The snorkel has an electric pump on the end, which sucks water into the tank.

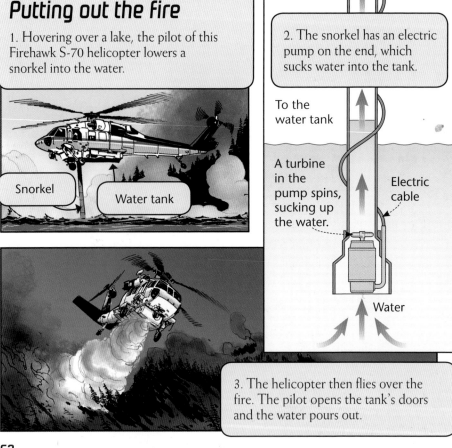

Snorkel

Water tank

To the water tank

A turbine in the pump spins, sucking up the water.

Electric cable

Water

3. The helicopter then flies over the fire. The pilot opens the tank's doors and the water pours out.

Here, a Bell 212 firefighter is working to put out a forest fire.

This large cabin can take firefighters and their equipment straight to a fire.

Water is scooped up from a lake into the bucket, then emptied over the fire.

The helicopter has a flexible bucket hanging down underneath it.

## Bell 212 (USA, 1968-present)

- **Length:** 17.43m (57ft)
- **Range:** 695km (432 miles)
- **Max. speed:** 259km/h (161mph)
- **Capacity:** 21 firefighters, including 1 pilot

# Police patrols

Police helicopters patrol busy cities. They can respond quickly to emergencies and help ground-based police with their operations – tracking down criminal suspects, chasing cars, and monitoring large crowds.

Video camera

Police in this helicopter are tracking a suspected stolen car speeding through city streets.

Pilot

Co-pilot

Observer's screen

Observer

Two observers sit in the back of the helicopter. They control a video camera as it zooms in on the car and driver. These images can be transmitted to police units across the city.

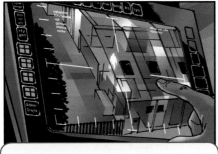

A red car is turning left onto Park Lane.

The crew use their radios to tell police on the ground which way the car is heading.

If the suspects escape from the car and try to hide...

...a thermal imaging camera locates them by detecting their body heat.

Then, a powerful searchlight helps to show where the suspects are.

# To the rescue

Helicopters can rescue people in areas that would be difficult to reach by car, plane or boat. The crew is trained to give emergency medical treatment.

This Agusta AW109K2 helicopter is designed for mountain rescue. It is about to pick up an injured walker from snow-covered mountains in Japan.

Tail skid stops the tail rotor from hitting rocks if the helicopter flies too close to a mountain.

## Agusta AW109K2 (England/Italy, 1995-present)

- **Length:** 13m (42ft)
- **Range:** 964km (599 miles)
- **Max. speed:** 285km/h (177mph)
- **Capacity:** 3 crew, 7 passengers and 1 stretcher

Tough, frost-resistant rotors and fuselage prevent the helicopter from being damaged in extreme cold or at high altitude.

Winch

Pilots are trained to fly and land in dangerous conditions, such as ice and fog.

富山県警

つるぎ

Wide and spacious cabin for carrying injured passengers

This member of the rescue crew is using hand signals to direct the helicopter pilot.

# Trouble at sea

Air-sea rescue teams are on-call 24 hours a day, using helicopters to search for and pick up people who have had an accident at sea.

This AW 139 helicopter is rescuing someone from the sea.

The rescuer, or winchman, collects the person using a harness.

Cable

Ripples in the water are caused by the *downwash* (gust of wind) from the main rotor.

## AgustaWestland AW139 (UK/Italy, 2003-present)

- **Length:** 16m (54ft)
- **Range:** 1061km (573 miles)
- **Max. speed:** 310km/h (193mph)
- **Crew:** 2

# Search by radar

Flying above stormy seas, it can be hard for the rescue team to see anything in the water. So, they search with radar. Radar uses signals to detect far-away objects...

...such as a boat in trouble.

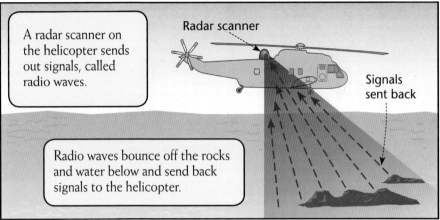

A radar scanner on the helicopter sends out signals, called radio waves.

Radar scanner

Signals sent back

Radio waves bounce off the rocks and water below and send back signals to the helicopter.

Different objects bounce back different signals. This information is shown on a screen.

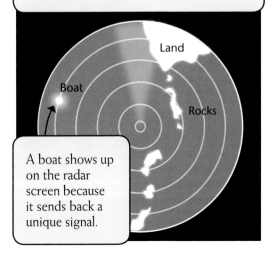

Land

Boat

Rocks

A boat shows up on the radar screen because it sends back a unique signal.

The helicopter flies to the boat and hovers above it, winching the crew to safety.

# Ambulance in the air

Air ambulances take people to hospitals in busy cities, where a traffic jam might slow down a road-based ambulance and put the patient's life at risk.

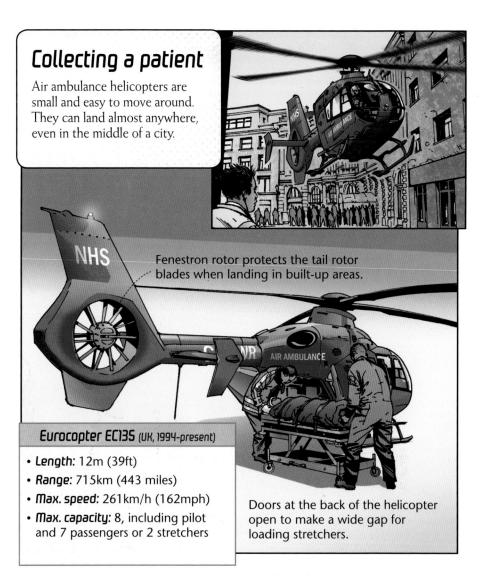

## Collecting a patient

Air ambulance helicopters are small and easy to move around. They can land almost anywhere, even in the middle of a city.

Fenestron rotor protects the tail rotor blades when landing in built-up areas.

### Eurocopter EC135 (UK, 1994-present)

- **Length:** 12m (39ft)
- **Range:** 715km (443 miles)
- **Max. speed:** 261km/h (162mph)
- **Max. capacity:** 8, including pilot and 7 passengers or 2 stretchers

Doors at the back of the helicopter open to make a wide gap for loading stretchers.

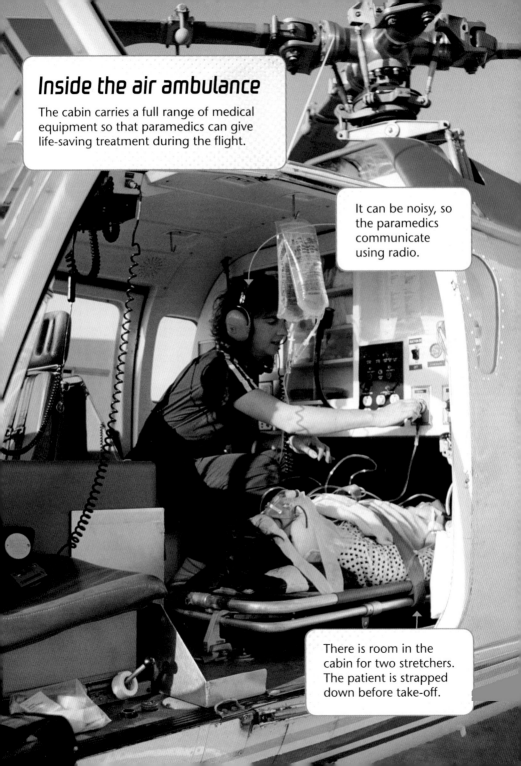

# Inside the air ambulance

The cabin carries a full range of medical equipment so that paramedics can give life-saving treatment during the flight.

It can be noisy, so the paramedics communicate using radio.

There is room in the cabin for two stretchers. The patient is strapped down before take-off.

# How does a helicopter fly?

The movement and shape of a helicopter's rotor blades are what lift up the helicopter and make it fly. Each one is curved on top and flatter underneath.

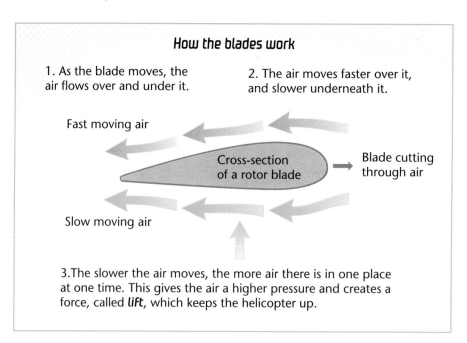

### How the blades work

1. As the blade moves, the air flows over and under it.

2. The air moves faster over it, and slower underneath it.

Fast moving air

Cross-section of a rotor blade

Blade cutting through air

Slow moving air

3. The slower the air moves, the more air there is in one place at one time. This gives the air a higher pressure and creates a force, called **lift**, which keeps the helicopter up.

## Helicopter controls

The pilot controls the main rotor using the collective and cyclic sticks.

Cockpit

**Collective stick**
Changes the angle of the main rotor blades to make the helicopter go up and down.

**Cyclic stick**
Tilts the whole of the main rotor, to make the helicopter go forwards, back and sideways.

# Collective stick

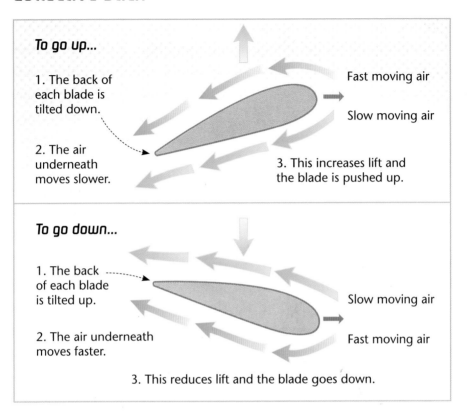

**To go up...**

1. The back of each blade is tilted down.

Fast moving air

Slow moving air

2. The air underneath moves slower.

3. This increases lift and the blade is pushed up.

**To go down...**

1. The back of each blade is tilted up.

Slow moving air

2. The air underneath moves faster.

Fast moving air

3. This reduces lift and the blade goes down.

# Cyclic stick

**To go forwards...**

...the whole of the main rotor is tilted forwards.

Nose tilts down.

**To go backwards...**

...the whole of the main rotor is tilted back toward the tail.

Nose tilts up.

**To go sideways...**

...the whole of the main rotor is tilted to one side or the other.

Helicopter will move this way.

# What does the tail rotor do?

The tail rotor keeps the helicopter's body, or fuselage, pointing straight. Without it, the main rotor would make the fuselage spin out of control.

Unlike planes, helicopters can stay in exactly the same place in the air. This is called hovering.

### How the rotors work together

Tail rotor

1. The main rotor spins around this way.

2. This applies a force called torque to the fuselage, making it spin around in a circle, the opposite way.

3. But, as the tail rotor spins, it acts against the torque, forcing the fuselage to go straight ahead.

# Rotating

The tail rotor can also be used to steer the helicopter left or right – or even make it spin 360° on the spot. The pilot controls the tail rotor using the yaw pedals.

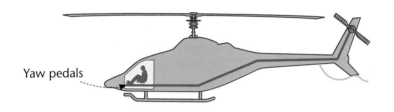

Yaw pedals

## Turning left and right

1. Flying straight: the pilot makes the tail rotor blades vertical.

Fuselage points forward.

Tail rotor

Direction of main rotor

Direction fuselage turns

2. Turning right: the pilot tilts the back of each rotor blade slightly away from the tail.

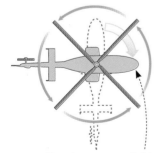

Fuselage turns right.

3. Turning left: the pilot tilts the back of each rotor blade slightly towards the tail.

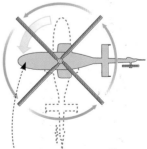

Fuselage turns left.

# Engine power

A helicopter's engine generates power to turn strong metal rods, called *shafts*, connected to the main and tail rotors. As the shafts turn, they make the rotors spin around.

If a helicopter's engine fails, the pilot can use the rotors to glide safely to the ground.

## How the engine powers the rotors

The engine burns jet fuel to generate power. Power is transferred from the engine, along the power shaft, to the gearbox, then onto the tail and main rotor drive shafts.

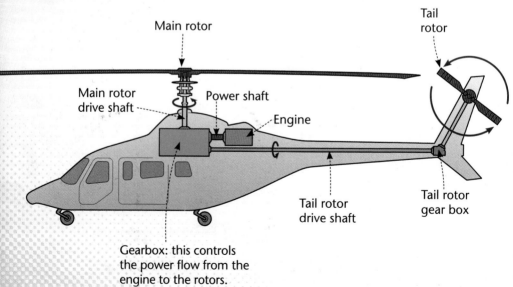

Main rotor

Tail rotor

Main rotor drive shaft

Power shaft

Engine

Tail rotor drive shaft

Tail rotor gear box

Gearbox: this controls the power flow from the engine to the rotors.

# How the engine works

Helicopter engines, called turboshafts, are small and light yet very powerful. They work using high-pressure air and burning fuel.

### Diagram of a turboshaft engine

**1** Air is sucked into the engine and through the compressor. This increases its pressure.

**2** The high-pressure air flows into the combustion chamber.

**3** Fuel is pumped into the combustion chamber. As the fuel mixes with the air it burns, and forms expanding gases.

Direction of air

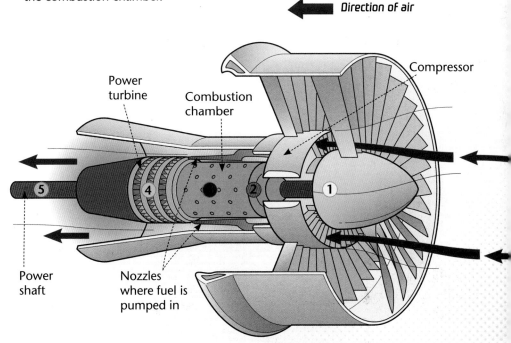

Power turbine

Combustion chamber

Compressor

Power shaft

Nozzles where fuel is pumped in

**4** The gases are forced out at high speeds through a power turbine, making it spin around very quickly.

**5** The spinning turbine makes the power shaft spin.

This is a Westland Gazelle
SA342. It is doing a spin
stunt, where the pilot
turns off the engine and
rolls, nose down, to the
ground, landing safely.

Smoke generators
blow out orange
smoke to make a
pattern across the sky.

# Spectacular stunts

Some helicopters can perform stunts to entertain crowds at air shows. The helicopters have powerful engines and light fuselages, so they're easy to move around.

Here are some of the stunts you might see:

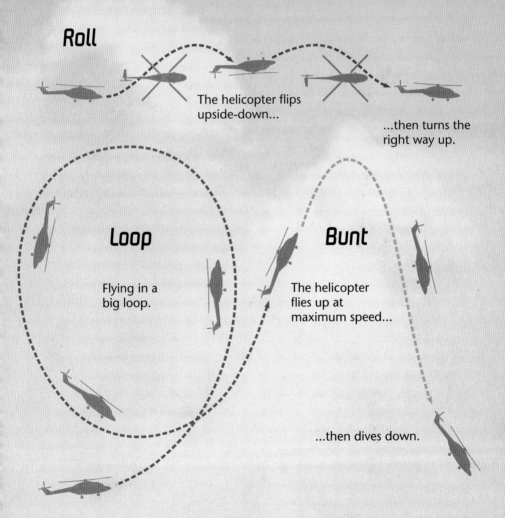

### Roll

The helicopter flips upside-down...

...then turns the right way up.

### Loop

Flying in a big loop.

### Bunt

The helicopter flies up at maximum speed...

...then dives down.

# Helipads and heliports

In cities, helicopters usually land in designated areas called helipads. Helipads are always marked by a white 'H' that is visible from the air.

This AW139 helicopter is landing on a helipad on top of a building in Hong Kong. People can hire the helicopter to take them to nearby cities.

B-MHJ

SKY SHUTTLE
空中快線

Cabin for up to 12 passengers

Maximum weight allowed is shown on the helipad. 10 = 10,000kg (22,000lbs)

H
10

# Heliports

Small airports specially for helicopters are called heliports. As well as one or more helipads, they have a control tower.

Control tower

B-MJH requesting permission to land.

The pilot contacts a controller using his headset, and asks permission to land.

Inside the control tower, air traffic controllers coordinate the movement of helicopters. Using radar, the controllers can see what other air traffic is in the area.

B-MJH, this is control tower, stand by.

Permission to land granted.

When it is safe, they give the pilot clearance to land the helicopter.

# Early designs

For thousands of years, people have experimented with making things fly using different types of rotors.

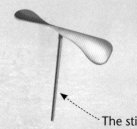

### Taketonbo 'Bamboo Dragonfly'
(Ancient China, about 2,500 years ago)

In Ancient China, children played with a bamboo toy, called a taketonbo. When the blades spun around, the toy flew through the air.

The stick was rolled between two hands.

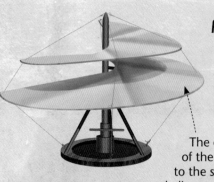

### Aerial screw (Italy, 1493)

Italian artist, Leonardo da Vinci, sketched out designs for a flying screw. But scientists now know his designs wouldn't have worked, as the screw couldn't spin fast enough.

The curved surface of the screw is similar to the shape of a helicopter's rotor blade.

Blades attached to 'wheels'

Engine

### Flying bicycle (France, 1907)

A flying bicycle, built by Paul Cornu, was the first helicopter to fly with a pilot. But it only managed to hover 30cm (2ft) off the ground for 30 seconds.

# Oehmichen No.2 (France, 1922)

In 1922, the Oehmichen No.2 flew for a minute and a half. By 1924, this helicopter had made a journey of just over 1.5km (just under a mile) and rose to 15m (50ft). It never flew further than this, so no more Oehmichens were made.

Four rotors lifted up the helicopter.

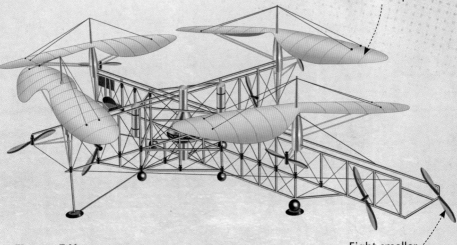

# Cierva C.4 (Spain, 1923)

The Cierva C.4, built by Juan de la Cierva, used an engine to push the helicopter forward. Wind rushing through the rotors made them turn, creating lift.

Eight smaller rotors were used for steering.

Single main rotor on top for the first time.

Tail 'rudder' for steering

Propeller powered by engine

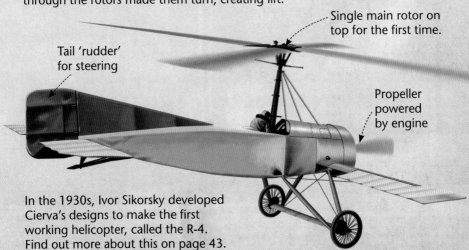

In the 1930s, Ivor Sikorsky developed Cierva's designs to make the first working helicopter, called the R-4. Find out more about this on page 43.

# Helicopters on the internet

There are lots of websites with information about helicopters. At the Usborne Quicklinks Website, you'll find links to some great sites where you can:

- See inside helicopters used by the emergency services.
- Watch search and rescue teams in action.
- Find out more about how helicopters are used on the battlefield.
- Take a virtual tour of famous attack helicopters, past and present.

For links to websites all about helicopters, go to the Usborne Quicklinks Website at **www.usborne-quicklinks.com** and enter the keyword **helicopters**.

This is what the co-pilot would see when flying a Bell 206B helicopter. The cockpit is covered by a glass 'bubble' so you can see above and below the helicopter, too.

# Glossary

This glossary explains some of the words used in this book. If a word is written in *italic* type, it has an entry of its own.

**ASW** Anti-Submarine Warfare helicopter, built to detect and attack submarines.

**attack helicopter** A military helicopter, armed with weapons for fighting enemy troops and vehicles.

**boom** The long part of the tail that keeps the *tail rotor* away from the *main rotor*.

**cabin** The space behind the *cockpit* where passengers and cargo are carried.

**cannon** A weapon that fires out *shells*.

**cargo** The goods or equipment a helicopter carries.

**chaff** A cloud of metal or glass fragments fired out by a helicopter to confuse *radar* systems.

**cockpit** The compartment where the *pilot* controls the helicopter.

**collective stick** The control in the *cockpit* that makes the helicopter fly up and down.

**cyclic stick** The control in the *cockpit* that makes the helicopter fly forward, back, or to the side.

**depth charge** An explosive set to go off when it reaches a certain depth in the sea.

**dipping sonar** A method for detecting submarines using sound, and the name for the equipment used for this.

**downwash** The stong gust of wind made by a helicopter's *main rotor*.

**drive shaft** The metal rod that turns a helicopter's rotors.

**exhaust** The hot, waste gases pumped out of a helicopter's engine.

**fenestron** A helicopter's *tail rotor* that is enclosed in the tail, to protect it from damage in built-up areas.

**flares** Pieces of hot metal fired out by a helicopter to attract heat-seeking *missiles* – and stop them from hitting the helicopter.

**fuselage** The body of a helicopter.

**gearbox** Device that controls the amount of power that goes from the engine to the rotors.

**GPS** Global Positioning System, a system for navigation using satellites.

**Gulf War** The name for the war between Iraq and other countries, including the USA, from 1990-1991.

**gunner** The crew member of a helicopter who aims and fires weapons.

**helipad** A landing area specially built for helicopters.

**heliport**  An airport for helicopters.

**hovering**  When a helicopter stays in exactly the same place in the air while it's still flying.

**Korean War**  The war, from 1950-1953, between the Republic of Korea (South Korea), supported by the USA, and the Democratic People's Republic of Korea (North Korea), supported by the USSR.

**lift**  A force that raises up a helicopter and keeps it in the air.

**main rotor**  Type of fan on the top of a helicopter's *fuselage* that spins around very fast, lifting the helicopter off the ground and moving it through the air.

**missile**  A weapon that uses its own engine and guidance system to fly to a target. It explodes on impact.

**Nap of the Earth (NoE)**  Flying close to the ground to avoid detection by *radar*.

**power shaft**  Where power is transferred from a helicopter's engine to its *gearbox*.

**radar**  A technology that uses radio waves to locate faraway objects, such as enemy aircraft.

**range**  The furthest distance a helicopter can fly without stopping to refuel.

**rocket**  A weapon that is fired toward a target using a *rocket launcher*. It explodes on impact.

**rocket launcher**  Tubes where *rockets* are stored and launched from.

**rotor blades**  Long, thin wings that make up a helicopter's rotor.

**Second World War**  The military conflict from 1939-1945 that affected most of the world's nations.

**shell**  An explosive fired out by a *cannon*.

**skids**  Ski-like supports underneath a helicopter.

**stub wing**  Short wing on each side of an *attack helicopter* for carrying weapons.

**tail rotor**  Type of fan on a helicopter's tail to control *torque*, and keep the *fuselage* pointing straight.

**tandem cockpits**  When two cockpits are positioned one in front of the other, usually in *attack helicopters*.

**tandem rotors**  Two *main rotors* positioned at either end of a helicopter's *fuselage*.

**torque**  A force that makes a helicopter's *fuselage* spin in the opposite direction to its *main rotor*.

**Vietnam War**  The war between the armies of North and South Vietnam that lasted from 1955-1975. The USA supported the South, and the USSR supported the North.

**yaw pedals**  Controls in the *cockpit* that steer the helicopter left and right by changing the *pitch* of the *tail rotor blades*.

# Index

Page numbers marked with an 'a' are found underneath the flap on that page.

# Acknowledgements

Every effort has been made to trace and acknowledge ownership of copyright. If any rights have been omitted, the publishers offer to rectify this in any future editions following notification. The publishers are grateful to the following individuals and organizations for their permission to reproduce material on the following pages: (t=top, b=bottom)

**cover** © AgustaWestland; **p1** © Don Farrall/Photolibrary; **p2-3** © David B. Fleetham/ Oxford Scientific/Photolibrary; **p10-11** © Art Tech/Aerospace Publishing (SH-3 Sea King); **p12-13** © AgustaWestland; **p14-15** © Louie Psihoyos/Corbis; **p15a** © Eric de Best/www.cockpits.net (Apache cockpit interior images); **p15ab** © Osprey Publishing Ltd. (overhead view of Apache AH-64); **p16** © Art Tech/Aerospace Publishing (MI-24 Hind and KA-50 Black Shark); **p21** © Franck Robichon/epa/Corbis; **p25, 26-27, p35t, p46-47** U.S. military helicopter photos provided courtesy of the U.S. Department of Defence. Use does not imply or constitute U.S. DoD endorsement; **p30-31** © Austin J. Brown LBIPP/www.aviationpictures.com; **p32-33** UK MOD Crown Copyright 2011; **p36-37** © U.S. Navy - digital vision copy/Science Faction/Corbis; **p38t** © Christian Wolff, www.radartutorial.eu; **p44-45** © J. Baylor Roberts/National Geographic Society/ Corbis; **p46b** © Osprey Publishing Ltd. (Bell UH-1 Iroquois); **p50-51** © Sikorsky Aircraft Corporation 2011. All rights reserved.; **p53** © Kai Fosterling/epa/Corbis; **p56-57** © Austin J. Brown LBIPP/www.aviationpictures.com; **p58** © AgustaWestland; **p61** © PhotoLink/Getty; **p64** © AgustaWestland; **p68** © AgustaWestland/www. aviationpictures.com; **p70** © AgustaWestland; **p74-75** © Austin J. Brown LBIPP/ www.aviationpictures.com.

Additional editorial material by Gill Doherty
Series editor: Jane Chisholm  Series designer: Zoe Wray
Digital design by John Russell
Additional illustration by Zoe Wray